To Be Human – Always

A Collection of Poems and Writings

Books by Tiffany Sunday

Poetry
Proper Grey Areas
Insatiable Consumption of Being

Nonfiction
How Dyslexics Will Rule the Future
Dyslexia's Competitive Edge
You Posted What!?

To Be Human – Always

A Collection of Poems and Writings

Tiffany Sunday

Tilton House Press
Dallas, Texas

Contents

Introduction – Know Thy Self   8

Beyond Limits   13

Hope   14

We Are Human   15

Bare   16

A Cat Won't Do   17

Weathered Stone   18

I Am Woman   19

Moonbeams   20

The Sun's Offer   21

Slice   22

Courage to Be   23

Open Road   24

Scab   25

No Longer Silent   26

Never Grey   27

Singular Promise to Be   28

Love Mystery   29

Unsure   30

Frozen   31

I Miss You   33

Digital Addiction   34

Nothing of Her   35

No Boxes   36

No Wake   37

South Wind   38

Bliss	39
Poetic Freedom	40
Glass Cage	41
A Leaf	42
Forever Waiting	43
God	44
Tick... Tock	45
Moon Love	46
Water	47
Human Brain	48
Sanity	50
Summer Night	51
Trees	52
Snow	53
Dirt	54
Memory Threads	55
Judgment	56
Longing	57
Daybreak	58
Confinement	59
The Eyes of My Soul	60
Too Much of You	62
Running	63
Today Becomes Tomorrow	64
Raw	65
Evaporation of Hate	66
New Dog	67
Living to Give Up the Dead	68
Do I Need a Drink?	69

Raindrops	70
Waiting	71
Democracy	72
Goodbye to Humanity	73
Sorrow	75
My Soul's Demands	76
Elimination	77
Earl Grey	78
Shared Experiences	79
I Write	80
Brick Wall	81
Fantasy	82
Evening Sky	83
Crows	84
Lightning Bug Tango	85
Digital Rodents	86
Pilot Light	87
False October	88
Chameleon	89
The Ocean Waves	90
Writings	92
Destination Unknown	98
1300 Miles to Barstow	101
The Rediscovery of Me	103
Poetry in the Wild	104
Acknowledgements	105
About the Author	106

Introduction – Know Thy Self

With each book, I evolve as an author. Books are a conduit for self-discovery and personal therapy. Our soul's characteristics are revealed as we transform raw creative energy into word art. Since *Proper Grey Areas*, I have been thinking about what it is to be human. It seems that with each social media post we become further removed from what feeds our soul and gives life meaning. By constantly living in the lives of others, we have little time for self-reflection for our own journey.

A couple of years ago, I toyed with the idea of writing a social science book about the impacts of technology on humanity and creativity. The phrase "To Be Human" rolled around in my thoughts for days as I considered the idea. However, regardless of my interest in the topic, I could not find it in my heart to write another nonfiction book about technology.

Instead, I focused on writing poetry and fiction. The awareness granted from writing three poetry books has changed who I am as a person. Our personal journeys provide insight and a heightened level of interpersonal understanding. Before I wrote *To Be Human,* I believed our personal journeys were centered on building spiritual connections between our souls and the Universe or personal religion of choice. Since then, I learned that understanding our individual work styles and dominant archetypes are equally important. When these parts of our personality are out of sync with our minds, hearts, and souls we become frustrated. This feeling of frustration is our intuition telling us to step back and find a pathway that will reconnect all these parts.

Two of my all-time favorite books are *Archetypes* by Caroline Myss, which I recommend frequently, and *Work Simply* by Carson Tate. Earlier this year, I realized I cannot ignore my Visionary Archetype as it defines every aspect of my life, work, and worldview. In Tate's book, she discusses common work styles and their corresponding traits. Tate highlights strengths and pet peeves for each work style. She offers readers a road map to follow that helps them focus on areas where they are most effective and identify work areas they should avoid. Too many times, we listen to others who seek to convince us to go against our natural archetypes and personalities. These individuals believe we can change or alter what is ingrained in our DNA by "faking it," "learning to like it," or worse, "giving it more time." We know instinctively when something is not working. Our intuition is very good at letting us know when we have gone off course. Listening to our gut and trusting its messages is crucial to avoid going down the wrong path.

Before I gained this awareness, I was frustrated both as a writer and strategist (my other work). I was so focused on forcing my Artist Archetype to dominate and to be *The One*, I did not realize I was creating my own internal conflict. If the Visionary was first, I thought I would have to do something else and give up writing. Thinking all or nothing was uncommon for me and was influenced by family members who believed writing books was a hobby and not a real profession. The duality forced me to peel back all the layers and see that being a Visionary gives my life purpose. The feeling of liberation was instant.

How I use my Visionary Archetype is up to me and no one else. A Visionary gives life to ideas. These ideas can be new books, business ventures, processes, songs, plays, or building designs. In stepping back and listening to my internal guidance, I finally see how all the pieces fit together. I feel relief that I can *be* both Visionary and Artistic. The most exciting part of the process is that I have told no one until now.

We are at our best when we understand our archetype's purpose and how it aligns with our natural talent and work style. Our purpose must also align with our heart and soul. With this awareness, I make decisions that are consistent with who I am. I allocate my time and energy to priorities while steering clear of toxic situations.

My personal journey continues as I work on my next book. I believe poetry and all art forms flow effortlessly, much like water from a faucet. Our art is natural. Mother Nature does not judge a tree and ask if the leaves are pretty enough for the forest or question whether it has used the right color of green. Instead, Nature allows trees to produce the leaves they believe will work best without interruption and judgment. As artists, we must produce art that is innate.

As artists, authors, and poets, we are responsible for capturing the beauty and essence of poetry (art), to tweak just enough but never overedit. Human creativity is a gift from God or the Universe, free from all encumbrances, a natural expression of humanity.

To Be Human – Always is a celebration of human creativity. It focuses on capturing the beauty of art for the love of art instead of superficial approval. The book is also a cautionary reminder of how easily our humanity and creativity can slip away under the weight of our technology. Similar to my previous poetry collections, this book contains nature-themed poems and a mix of eclectic poetry reflecting life's rawness, human emotions, and the joys of being.

Beyond Limits

The womb of comfort
crumbled
as the world I knew
disappeared,
evaporated from memory.

Fear become an intimate friend
pushing my capacity to cope
beyond my limits,
stripping any remaining
hope,
while simultaneously destroying
the ability to return to the past,
leaving normalcy forever in its wake.

Hope

We stare in disbelief,
not knowing if the line will hold.
Hope,
held by a fragile tread,
holds us together,
taut,
pulled by both sides.

Suddenly, without warning,
the thread falls to the ground,
leaving us separated in silence as Hope
disappears.

We Are Human

To be human is to feel and respect our emotions.

To be human is to gain wisdom from experience and be willing to step out from the crowd.

To be human is to partake in the simplest of joys without judgment.

To be human is to willingly listen to another's hopes, desires, and dreams.

To be human is to celebrate the best of our authentic selves.

Bare

Bare.
Only the bark
exposed to the bitter cold,
waiting for the sun to shine again.
Without a blanket of leaves
to protect me,
waiting
patiently for the sun
to come and warm me.

A Cat Won't Do

"A cat won't do if you want a dog,"
he said, staring down at the empty pet
carrier.
"A cat will leave you wanting more
if your heart is set on a dog.
"I've seen this before," he said.
"People settle for something
they don't want
when they should have waited.
"The wrong decision leaves them in a
bad way.
"Always accepting something else,
something less
than their hearts' desire.
"Too afraid to go against the flow of
others
when the heart longs to make a decision
to step outside external control.
"Better to wait and get yourself a dog,
'cause a cat just won't do.
A cat will leave you wanting a dog...."

Weathered Stone

Lost in the forest
I step on a stone
broken by time,
which reminds me of you,
buried in the dirt,
covered by moss and leaves
beneath the trees.

I stare at a stone
weathered by time
a memory of you
bringing the past to the present
ashes to life
and back to dirt again.

I Am Woman

Before I could read,
her voice filled my ears,
taught my soul to believe
all things were possible,
because I was to be a woman
without limits,
without boundaries.

Her words flow through my being
words of encouragement,
words of wisdom
to face the challenges ahead,
for I am Woman.

Moonbeams

Moonbeams
comfort my soul.
A gentle blanket of light flowing from
the heavens,
smoothing away the day's raw edges.

The Sun's Offer

The Sun, a burning orb of fire, sat down
next to me.
Side by side, we contemplated the
future.
I wondered why,
the Sun befriended me
on that cold windy day.
Why did he choose to sit with me?
I waited, as we gazed toward the empty
landscape,
for an answer
to make the world right again.
After a while,
the Sun said, "It's been a long day. It's
time for bed, to lay to rest another day."
"Will you be back tomorrow?" I asked.
"Yes, I'm always here when you need a
friend to bring light to darkness,
give warmth when it's cold.
I'll always be here
to start a new day
when all is possible again."

Slice

You slice my soul
on a chopping block.
Slowly, I watch you eat the tiny parts of
my being with a fork.

Before you finish,
I reach from behind,
striking you down,
ending your abuse forever.

Courage to Be

The courage to be me
feels as foreign as a distant land
across the sea,
an unfamiliar place that I have yet to see.

The courage I seek lies
beyond the horizon,
along the miles of hidden roads
that have yet to experience my
footsteps.

A decision must be made,
stay and become one with groupthink,
or pack my gear,
let go of the fear,
and walk along the roads I have yet to
travel.

Open Road

The road beckons,
calls for me to join
the open miles ahead.
The road knows
more than I.

Hundreds of miles of wisdom
bestowed on those
willing to listen,
willing to go the distance,
willing to take the time
to learn.

The open road beckons
my soul once again.

Scab

I pick at a scab on my knee
until it bleeds.
The flowing blood is a secret
buried deep within
that needs to be revealed.

When the pain of silence becomes too
intense,
burning a hole through my soul,
shooting up from my remaining core,
I remove the scab
for instant relief
as pain races out the door.

No Longer Silent

No longer will you weaponize
my words against me,
firing angry statements
across my body,
across my soul
to tear down
the very essence of me.

No longer silent,
armed with defenses of what you fear
most,
for the Truth is loud,
loud enough to drown out your lies,
raining down like bombshells
forming debris piles at my feet.

Never Grey

Black or white
is the foundation of your decisions.
Yes or no,
never willing to meet partway,
you delete the middle ground,
eliminate compromise.
Light or dark
never sunrise or sunset
always one, never two.

Black or white
you or me
never together
always binary,
leaving us stationary,
anchored
on a boat
floating upon a sea of inflexibility.
Love or hate,
all or nothing.
Singular,
missing middle ground.
Always one or the other,
never together.

Singular Promise to Be

The singular promise to be me
to be my own person is unnatural in the
eyes of others.

The courage to be different,
seems as far away
as a distant planet.

Dare I change?
Travel undiscovered miles,
take steps in a new direction
to fulfill the promise I made to myself,
so that I can be me?

Love Mystery

Your love is steady
within the chaos
always present
even when you're not around.

Your love is constant,
offering gentle words on a tough day
when a smile can't be found.
A reaffirming hug
when the dam needs a plug.

Your love is a mystery
of how I found you
and you found me
on the island of lost souls
floating at sea.
Just you and me,
together
forever.
Your love is a mystery.

Unsure

How do you sleep at night?

Injustice flows from your fingertips
flooding others,
digging a grave of despair.

How do you sleep at night?

A soul rotten to the core,
with death at your feet,
lies flow from your forked tongue.

How can you sleep at night?

Frozen

Freezing cold weather
chilled us to the bone.
Some claimed
they never saw the cold air coming.
The debate is all but forgotten
as we burn our belongings for survival.

A record-breaking winter vortex,
swept across the land,
removing modern luxuries of society,
leaving us with no plan
as we resume a place in history before
plumbing and electricity.

Shocked, mad, and frozen
are we
with no mobile app to save us
no just-in-time food delivery to feed us.

Without instant digital solutions,
despair grows as relief from our freezing
environment is not forthcoming.
Others watch from outside the invisible
boundary

as news reports spread across the
airwaves
of parents tossing their children's toys
onto the flames to melt the ice away.

The demands for action rise like hot
flames,
almost hot enough to thaw the freeze,
revealing the ill planning of others.

The heat faded as quickly as it rose,
leaving everyone where they were
before – *frozen*.

I Miss You

I miss you.

I can't stand the loss,
can't stand the pain
as I watch you slip away.

I miss you.

You leave;
my world forever changes
leaving happiness at the gate.

I wave goodbye
to yesterday's memories
trigging an avalanche of longing
so deep,
it touches the earth's core.

I miss you.

I miss our time together.
Now, it feels like a dream
fading in and out of my memory.

I miss you.

Digital Addiction

Software dashboards
inducing hypnotic effect,
lost within the bits of data
worshiping the Social Media God.

Watching
creates a craving for the dopamine rush,
a fix of constant scrolling of likes.

The need to feed the desire intensifies.
Any post will do to feed the addiction,
good, bad, doesn't matter,
just keep the drug coming.

Need more to feed the addiction.
Click, like, scroll
the hours away.
Days pass without notice.
Humanity disappears.

Nothing of Her

I know nothing of her.
No permission was granted
on that cold winter day.

None.

I can say very little of her, her family, or
her relations.

Only that she continues to write,
drawing my attention
for reasons unknown.
As I said before, I know nothing of her.

No Boxes

No categories
no narrow views
no labels
no boxes to check.

Eliminate confinement
free to read and think
about new possibilities,
new opportunities
for the future
that are brighter than the past.

No Wake

Companies race across the digital ocean
in blinded bliss,
seeking corporate dominance,
leaving behind an unavoidable wake.

Little concern for humanity,
the race intensifies
as the rudders shred everything in their
path.

Advancement should never cost
anyone, or anything,
everything.

South Wind

South wind blowing from the sea
leaving nothing in between
except you and me.

Salty air whipping away words of love
that floated along like fairy tale dreams
you once told me.

Promises washed away by ocean spray,
like fairy dust
tossed to the wind,
spreading across the land
with the ease of your hand.

South wind blowing from the sea,
leaving nothing
of what was once you and me.

Bliss

Gone are the days of
pain
entrapment
sorrow
abuse
helplessness.
Gone is the never-ending cycle of
darkness.

Your healing warmth,
bright as the sun,
spreads across my landscape,
filling my heart with love
so tender
so true
so real.
Bliss is being in love with you.

Poetic Freedom

Without bounds
with the freedom to express
emotions that define humanity.

To feel alive
instead of tied down.

Poems must be set free
from the bonds of rhyming
and forced word symmetry.

Poems must be free to roam like you and
me.

Glass Cage

The digital thin surface
we race across,
instantly clicking away
the very essence
of who we are
to gain approval
while eliminating loneliness.

Silently,
our natural internal definition of self
evaporates into the digital dust
of the latest images
posted to the digital sphere.
Round and round
the invisible tail we chase,
never realizing
the hole we dig
to bury our humanity.

A Leaf

I was once a leaf
with knowledge from a tree,
who gently floated to the ground
reborn anew
to learn
the importance of life.

Growth requires time
sourced from within.
Contentment requires silencing the toxic
habitual voices.
Patience requires maturity.

Once I was a leaf
instructed to share the knowledge
I gained from a tree.

Forever Waiting

Sublime twinkling of lights
simple shadows of childhood
dreams of hope
wrapped in a red shirt,
snow-white beard
waiting patiently
excitement delayed.

God

God, help me to be me
instead of someone
I am forced to be.

God, help me
find the courage
to fulfill your purpose
when others disagree.

God, give me strength
when others choose otherwise
driven by determination
to change who I am
instead of what I am made to be.
Full of vision, ideas, and creativity.

God, give me the grace to
be the person you need me to be.

Tick... Tock

Every single month of the year
thousands of words are spoken without
meaning,
hundreds of emotions shared without
compassion.

Every single day of the month
the drama of others steals away
smiles, hugs, laughter, excitement, and
contentment.

Every single minute of the day
useless tasks are given
for the amusement of others,
spending priceless moments of
humanity.

Moon Love

Make love to me
under the evening moonlight,
caressed by summer's gentle breeze,
wrapped in your sweet perfection of
pure delight.

Water

Water drips at the edge
into a space unknown,
darkness
dripping
falling
into nowhere.

Tiny molecules of water
disappearing
from the present
into the past
forbidden from the future.

Water flows down the mountain
rushing across the landscape
taking away
everything that once was and never will
be.

Sweeping into the darkness,
destroying today, tomorrow, and
yesterday.
Water drips at my feet.

Human Brain

Disappearing daydreams
vanish into digital screens.
Technology eats away our neutrons
eliminating the ability
to create
to envision something new,
beyond the confines
of a tiny screen.

The brain froths and fits
like a chained animal,
longing to run unbridled in open space.
A constant perpetual craving
for mental freedom.
To chase dreams.
To believe in tomorrow,
grounded by the possibilities
crafted from the mind's eye.

Instead,
days upon on days, the brain chews
upon itself,
marinating in a pot of toxicity,
drowning in dated thoughts
and images,

creating a circular path of sameness,
etching a path to nowhere.

Round and round,
the same thoughts
are locked in place,
forming a wall,
preventing anything new from
anywhere.

Without imagination
stagnation forms
creating sameness
void of diversity.

Empty
nothingness
slowly destroys
any ounce of human creativity
remaining.

Sanity

Sanity breaks
just as the sun rises
across the sky.

Crazy thoughts dance within me
when I am with you.
Sanity is so fragile
when you are in love with one who
never sees two.

So many times,
I could have been sane.
Instead, I am crazy with you.

Sanity,
such a high price
to pay to be
with you.

Summer Night

Shadows of the night
dance with delight
beneath the moonlight
watching lightning bugs take flight
creating a heavenly sight.

Trees

Trees whisper
words of wisdom
flowing down the mountainside.

Snow

Waiting for snow
seems simple enough,
grey clouds
waiting in queue.

Upper system aloft
comes together in perfect formation.

Timing,
temperature,
moisture--
all together
with the singular goal of snow.

Dry ground
grey skies.
Sometimes,
Mother Nature
has other plans.

Dirt

The dirt is silent
as the moisture hangs in the wind,
tiny droplets of water
chasing after the sun,
driving the burning orb down into the
night.

Begging for the stars,
wishing for the moon.

No rain,
no gain,
leaving only the pain of the parched
earth.

The sun rises
in a cloudless sky
leaving the drought cycle on repeat.

Memory Threads

Memories wrapped by the tiny hands of
time,
secured with twine
so elusive
that it feels like yesterday.

Tangible feelings
disappear
into space.

Interwoven so delicately
into our cells,
triggering
biological responses
of moments from the past,
creating a longing
to return to where we once were...
before digital intrusion.

Judgment

The man judges from a cove,
peeling back all that is love.

Hidden away from the grasping arms
that reach out to capture
and harm.

Judgment flows,
flooding the empty spaces,
determined to hide the truth
while flushing reason to the sea.

Longing

Longing,
over and over.
Longing to be near
instead of far away.

The pain of being without you
grips, rips, and tears
leaving a scar across my soul.

Patched together with salted memories
are moments of darkness
interwoven with tiny rays of light
as I resume life again.

Daybreak

Silent
early morning
untouched perfection.

Solitude wrapped in a warm blanket
savoring the quietness
before decisions
before demands
brought about by another day.

Confinement

My soul
confined in a box for days
condensed into
to a small square
without light
without sound
without music.

Scraped
crawled
to escape
to be free
to dance
among the trees
to sing with the birds.

Instead, raw emotions
lay bare
tearing apart the fibers of my being.

My soul perseveres
after days of determination,
rendering everything else, except
freedom, an annoyance.

The Eyes of My Soul

The eyes of my soul
stare back at me,
demanding to be seen,
demanding action,
demanding to be human,
to be set free
from the insanity of sameness
of duplication of groupthink.

The eyes of my soul
stare back at me,
demanding to be heard,
demanding refusal of digital
assimilation,
demanding that I never forget I am
human first.

The eyes of my soul
demand justice,
ethics,
humility,
and the truth
in our slippery slope world.

The eyes of my soul
look at you
and demand to be heard,
demand to be seen as human,
instead of a passing digital image of
obscurity.

Too Much of You

Too much of you is not enough
too much of you is what I crave
too much of you is what I need
too much of you forever and ever.

Too much of you is the best of the
summer breeze.
Too much of you is better than anything
I can imagine beyond a picturesque
sunrise or sunset.
Too much of you is a perfect way to start
the morning or end the day.

Too much of you is where I always want
to be.

Running

Running away from today into
tomorrow where I need to be.

Running so far away from where you
wanted to keep me.

Running out of reach
going forward
leaving backward behind.

Running into the dawn of the new day,
leaving the dark of the night behind.

I run away from now into later
forgetting the day
dreaming about tomorrow.

I run into the sunset
to welcome the dawn of a new day.

Running liberates.

Today Becomes Tomorrow

Today becomes tomorrow
when yesterday is left behind
where we were once before.

So many stories,
so many things from the past
that seemed impossible once,
are easily cast aside.

Waiting for resolution
seems fruitless now
by mere constitution
of your indecisiveness
always parading on display,
waiting for my words to disappear
for new partner redistribution.

Raw

The pain cuts deep.
Escape seems impossible.
Your words spread fear
like a spam sandwich
past its expiration date.

So intense
the heat of your anger burns
through my skin
leaving a scar
that's difficult to hide.

Alone
sitting in the car,
rescue seems impossible.
No help from family.
Friends disappear
too much for a summer chat by the pool.

Your anger spreads
across the landscape
leaving nothing.
Silence begs for mercy.
Your mood passes
granting another day.

Evaporation of Hate

Say goodbye to yesterday,
hello to tomorrow,
only if hate is destroyed.

All we know
seems so far away
into next year.

Each day is strange,
stranger than before,
always on repeat,
over and over, same ole story.

Will we know when it's different?
Will we have time to change the course
of history?
Will we have time to destroy hate?

New Dog

"Get a new dog when the time is right,"
he said.
Waiting for a reply not received, he
continues.
"The grieving process takes time. You
need space to heal.
To create a place in your heart for the
new dog.
A dog that will become one with you,
like the dog before."
Nothing else is said
between us,
as the dog crate resumed its place in the
closet.

Living to Give Up the Dead

So many times, the living give up the
dead,
leaving dreams in the gutter,
seeking digital solitude
from far away,
far away from being human.

Emotions bleed to the floor.
Pools of blood of yesterday's ideas
drip down the stairs
draining the passion from life.
Dreams dying
without sunlight
of a promise
of tomorrow
or the future,
causing the soul
to withdraw
into the dark, damp cave of sorrow
only to watch humanity give up its dead.

Do I Need a Drink?

Maybe I need a drink
or perhaps I should write?
Either way, it's a battle
of two minds that appear as one.
I need to pay bills.
Instead, my soul whispers, "Write!"
Just a little more
just a few more words,
without worry until tomorrow
when bills are due.

My soul whispers, "Explore!"
Instantly, creativity pours onto the
keyboard,
filling the pages,
feeding my soul.
Hours of work go unnoticed
until the songs are sung
and the books are written,
so I write
while the bills wait.

Raindrops

Dancing upon raindrops
in a summer storm,
washing away the pain
formed long ago
as crusted plaque on the edges of my
soul,
destroyed by lightening
creating a clean,
fresh space
to breathe again.

Waiting

Waiting, waiting, waiting
on you again.
Time passes slowly
crawling across the horizon of humanity.

Waiting, waiting, waiting
again,
unsure when you will be
here, next to me.

Time moves slowly
ticktock
ticktock
watching the hands of time disappear
while I wait for you.

Democracy

Silence of the courtroom
broken only by the sound of pages being
turned.

Silence speaks louder than words
of men and women
waiting to serve.

Selected at random,
willing to do their part,
a gift from the past
in the name of democracy.

Goodbye to Humanity

"Sit down," he says.
"The bench is empty,
you see.
No one else
wants to talk
too busy with other things,
too busy to say hello."

"Oh, I am sorry. But I don't have time
either." I respond in a hurry.

"Everyone is staring down at their tiny
screens. Passing silently, they are
shocked when I speak."

"Please, sit down,"
he says, begging not for him,
but for all of us.
Each day on the boardwalk,
he watches us disappear with each
passing step.
"I don't understand,"
he says, and then continues.
"No one wants to talk,
text instead.

"Why would I text you
when you're sitting next to me,
lost within the silence
of digital nothingness,
of empty responses
easily forgotten?"

I give no reply.

"Please, I beg of you, please sit down and
visit," he says.

Sorrow

Sorrow drove east
leaving behind Sadness.
Sorrow sought relief amongst the leaf-
peeping tourists,
surrounded by beauty in all shapes and
colors,
a mosaic of God's design.

Sadness stayed behind,
unhappy,
unwilling to move forward,
resolved to wait for Sorrow's return.

My Soul's Demands

My soul said the other day, "How much longer will I be confined?"
"A few more days. I need to finish a project, a rather taxing project. Please be patient," I responded.

"I will, and then I will demand your attention. I am the keeper of human creativity and will raise holy hell if you resist!" my soul said.

Afterward, my soul and I sat in silence along the rocky shore, watching the waves crash over and over, thinking if we waited long enough, something new would appear.

Finally, as I watched the sun disappear into the ocean, my soul said, "We better go. We have lots of work to do."

Elimination

Brittle, burnt
corn husks stand tall
determination evident
hope prevailing
as clouds begin to form.

The remaining leaves hang on
praying to the God above.
One drop of rain
evaporates on impact
instantly eliminating the crops.

Earl Grey

Bitter cold arrived from Scotland
on a slow-moving train.
Scarfs and trench coats were the order
of the day.

Earl Grey steeped to perfection
to chase away the chill,
perfectly fitting for the remainder of the
day.

Shared Experiences

Shares stories,
shared experiences of laughter and pain.
Emptiness consumed my being
as the realization became unavoidably
evident.
We had nothing in common.

Time creates an illusion
of deep friendships,
family relations
only to mask the truth.

I don't know you.
You don't know me.
Sadly, the time spent together is the only
commonality between us.

I Write

I write
to be real
instead of words preformulated and
auto-filled.

I write
what I see,
smell, hear, taste, and feel
instead of what drives comments, clicks,
and likes.

I write
what my heart
longs to say
what my soul begs to live.

I resist conforming measure
prescribed by institutions focused on
digital structure and acceptance.

I write, like the others before me,
an authentic reflection of humanity.

Brick Wall

My writer's pen waits
in silence.
Stress stops the creative flow.
When words do appear,
they are choppy, forced, meaningless
chatter of social media sewage
unworthy of print.

Stressful decisions fill the cavities of my
creative landscape, leaving little room
for curious exploration.

Emptiness fills the space, leaving only
stillness.
My soul waits in despair.
Continuous cloudy sky accentuates the
situation;
Mother Nature has nothing to say,
leaving a grey background while the sun
has gone off to play.

A mosquito sucks blood from my foot--
a metaphor of the stress that is causing
the creative fluids to disappear from my
writer's pen.

Fantasy
Song Lyrics

Over winter break, my son's music
inspired these lyrics. Maybe someday, I
will find these lyrics a melody partner.

I'm fantasizin'
about big money and Vegas dreams
Rolly car
Lambo in every color
dreamin'
about big money
and Vegas dreams
no worries
no cares
plenty of money
in my pocket
bling for friends
I'm just dreamin'
of what life could be
living a Hollywood dream
all too soon, reality dulls my fantasy.

Evening Sky

To view the evening sky with human
eyes only,
without devices, filters,
soft hues of the nighttime clouds in
pinks, blues, and greys,
leisurely floating across the open sky
as they whisper, "Summer is here!"

Different from their winter cousins
so stark, bitter, and defined,
summer clouds
inspire moments of lazy afternoons,
restful days by the water, beach, or bay.

Softly these quiet airborne reminders in
multiple shades of color
float effortlessly by,
triggering
childhood memories of vacations along
the gulf shore filled with sandy toes,
sunburnt skin,
a feeling as real as the evening clouds in
the sky.

Crows

The Crows came by today
to investigate.
Chatter did they
of nonsense on a warm summer's day.

The Crows came by today
with so much to say.
The Blue Jays replied,
"Too much nonsense!"
"Too much noise!"
"Not enough wisdom."
The debate continued for hours
in the tall, majestic trees.

If the trees could talk,
what would they say?
Would they share their wisdom born of
time and resistance
or ignore the empty chatter of the Crows
and debating Blue Jays?

The trees said nothing.
The Crows came by today.

Lightning Bug Tango

Outside
summer evening perfection
lightning bugs dance the tango.

One, two, light up and go
tiny, synchronized movements across
the lawn.

One, two, light up and go
lightning bug tango
a beautiful dance under the moonlight.

Outside
lies summer perfection
without the glare of a screen.
Care to join me?

Digital Rodents

We scatter like rats,
hunting for sustainability
while vultures feast upon opossums
playing dead.

Digital illusions
transfer humans into passing sheep
as we search for authenticity
impossible to find.

Plenty of apps at our fingertips
to download and share
consuming time,
leading to nonsense,
coming up empty.

Racing through the streets,
clawing for humanity,
hunting for food,
hiding from cats
to avoid instant extinction.

Pilot Light

At birth,
our pilot light of creativity
is ignited,
a steady blue flame
burning bright
within us.

Without warning
a cold, digital,
brisk wind demands
group assimilation,
extinguishing the flame
for eternity.

False October

Green leaves remain
firmly attached
past their scheduled departure.

The calendar begs for fall
with each passing day of October.
The calendar demands the leaves to
change colors, drop, and comply.
The leaves respond, "No can do."

Chameleon

Red, yellow, blue, and green
Which color do you need me to be?
I can change for you,
I can change for them,
I can change on demand
and dance your color game.

With each shift in color
a tiny part of my soul
disappears
into the spinning color wheel
of forced entertainment.
Spinning,
spinning out of control,
unable to let go,
unable to save myself
I disappear.

The Ocean Waves

The waves watched him
walking along the shore.
For miles, the waves followed his
footsteps
only to wipe them away
with the gentle ebb and flow of the
ocean.

Writings

Destination Unknown

The pressure from family to write a novel and earn enough money to cover my bills and support my son at college is intense. The pressure, when applied by others, can produce a diamond from the constant compression of external forces. My family offers advice about the type of books I should write to earn the coveted status of a *New York Times* best-selling author. On other days, they advocate jobs for which I am overqualified. My experience and background never align to their suggested professions. Regardless of what I do, their support of my writing is absent.

Five years ago, I started writing a fiction manuscript entitled *Never Again, She Said.* The story is about a woman who discovers her husband cheating. Her family is unsupportive and believes the breakup is her fault not his. So far, I have written over 23,000 words. Ironically, since 2016, I have had three books published. One nonfiction and two poetry collections. This is the fourth book since I started writing *Never Again, She Said*. To anyone on the outside it is obvious that completing the fiction manuscript is not on my writing to-do list. I binge watch Netflix's shows and movies or write on new poetry instead of working on the novel. I am unsure if it is part of my defiance of refusing to give into my family's demands. The more they push me to write cheeky commercial fiction, the more I dive into poetry and soul-searching writings.

While editing this book, I wondered in an email to my editor, Cindy Vallar, if I should consider writing a personal discovery book similar to *Bird by Bird* by Anne Lamott. Another book that is a favorite of mine is *Simple Abundance* by Sarah Ban Breathnach. Cindy's support infused instant creativity and this writing was added last minute to this book as we prepared to go to press.

I've noticed a profound difference between writing about our natural journey and thinking of fiction dialog. My Visionary Archetype doesn't like tedious laborious tasks like characters talking. Also, my soul and brain love feasting on ideas and connecting unrelated dots, which is difficult to do in a novel unless you are writing a mystery, which doesn't interest me at all. I believe things happen for a reason, that the Universe provides guidance if we are willing to listen. Today, the message was to write about the journey and share my experiences with you.

The timing of my email conversation with Cindy and the demise of my air-conditioning unit are oddly inspiring. I have been defiant not to call a repair company because I know I will have to spend at least $6,000 to fix or replace the compressor. I do not want to spend that much money right now. To support my writing, I have also started another business that requires funding. Yes, it's a little warm in the house as summer refuses to leave in October. Living in the South, we never have a real fall; instead it's a just sample of autumn that individuals up north experience.

My new routine involves opening the windows in the morning and evenings to cool down the house, like my grandparents did for so many years without central air. In the past two weeks I have become more in sync with nature's gentle morning sunrises, and the cool evening breeze from the window fans. Forging air conditioning feels old school. Like the trend among college students called Light or Dark Academia. Either way, a few hours each day in the morning and evening, life feels like my early childhood before the chaos of digital technology arrived. Before social media we only knew about events that were happening in our small worlds. Now, we are expected to take on everyone's issues in addition to managing our problems. Not to be callous or uncaring, but it's important to recognize the mental burden social media can place on us as we scroll through our digital devices.

Something is changing within me because of my new routine. As a Visionary, I connect ideas. If this small writing piece grows into a book, you and I will learn how my decision to delay the AC unit repairs changed my perspective; I know it is already happening now as I write.

As I mentioned in an earlier paragraph, "Destination Unknown" was inspired by Cindy. I am also testing the idea of writing a book by the same title. A book that would focus on our personal journey of life, work, and writing. As I worked on the first chapter of this potential new book, I felt an overwhelming sense of guilt that I should be doing something else instead of writing. That my actions should focus on career activities that are more profitable, more worthy of my time than a useless hobby. The guilt during the thirty minutes of writing was almost unbearable. The message I have received for most of my life has been clear: do anything, except writing! To write is an act of defiance and is probably the underlying reason why I am not fixing my AC either.

My soul refuses to write anything cheap just to sell something. I've sold out so many times in the past, I can't anymore especially with my writing. I have discovered that writer's block occurs when we feel forced to write content that is contradictory to our soul's desire. When we write to appease others, the creativity stops cold, and writing feels like a form of punishment instead of an expression of art.

Each time we sell a piece of our soul, it gets more difficult to reclaim what we gave away. Carolyn Myss, one of my all-time favorite authors, writes in *Sacred Contracts*, "that when you do not seek or need external approval, you are at your most powerful." I can't sell out my soul anymore as I am afraid that I may not have much of my soul left to give away to individuals who could care less what they take from others. The AC has become a sort of symbol, a rallying call to protect my writer's soul. To write for the love of writing instead of the need for external approval. But standing tall against the negativity of others hasn't been easy. I have been to hell and back a couple of times and am tired of visiting the same demeaning location. I am wiser, more compassionate, and much more protective of my soul because of my life experiences.

Cindy's words of encouragement unexpectedly opened the creativity floodgates and the words jumped for joy and appeared as easily on the page as their poetry cousins. Her words offered permission to pursue a book idea I have been considering for years. I have been reluctant to write a personal journey book for fear of what others would think and the exposure of having my soul out there for all the world to view.

For authors, it feels like the world sees our soul each time our work is published. The most difficult decisions we make as artists is to select the unknown path. To go against the grain and discover who we are as a person. Why do we need to know where we are going each and every day? The joy of life is the discovery of the tiny bits and pieces along the way. The moments we keep to ourselves and store in the treasure box of our being. To be recalled from memory to ease the stress and pain of navigating life.

As much as my soul seeks to write this morning, to explore the unknown, to view the turning leaves of New England, to bake pumpkin bread, I must return to work and the tasks on my to-do list while nurturing the dream that someday I will be able to write full time.

1300 Miles to Barstow

In August 2019, my son and I drove to California. The trip was a gift for his upcoming senior year in high school. The road trip struck a nerve within my soul, resulting in my transition to poetry from business writing. The trip inspired a title for a book. While we were driving home, I kept thinking *1300 Miles to Barstow*. As much as I liked the title, I have yet to create anything for it. This past week, I thought maybe *1300 Miles to Barstow* was a benchmark instead of a book. A point in time when I decided to change the course of my life.

The picture of Barstow, California that I took during our trip captured the vast expansive land with miles of desert. Nothing between me and the horizon. If I wanted, I could run for miles without encountering anything or anyone to say no to my ideas. I could be like Forrest Gump and *run* with curiosity fueling my legs.

The word "run" is a metaphor for how I felt that day, free from creative encumbrances. *1300 Miles to Barstow* has become a milestone, a phrase that will always remind me of the courage I found during our trip to shift the focus of my writing. The title also recalls cherished memories of the trip with my son. In Barstow, I committed myself to become the writer I always wanted to be.

The Rediscovery of Me

Somewhere between March and June, I found myself -- the real me who resides within my soul. The awareness came about without much fanfare from media, friends, or family. This awareness came from within and is not something I broadcast every day.

This new awareness is felt in my daily actions of honoring my priorities. I make sure that each day I focus on the things that matter most and work to eliminate the nagging, guilty feeling I am doing something wrong. During my daily runs, I remind myself that I can stand against the peer pressure of others and make a conscious effort to put my mental health needs first. In return, I make sure that I am aware of others and listen with the same respect I expect in return.

One of the changes I made was to run on the weekends at White Rock Lake, a small city lake near downtown. For years, I've wanted to run at this lake, but the option was not available due to parenting duties and work demands.

Now, I make the time to run along the shores of the lake on the weekends listening to the lapping waves and passing conversations. For an hour each Sunday, I mentally rest. My mind and soul instantly switch to vacation mode when I arrive at the lake and park the car. The surroundings and sounds perform a mental massage reducing stress as my thoughts disappear. I do not listen to anything. I run as free from technology as possible.

I think of the line in the movie *Holiday in the Wild*, where Kate responds to her soon-to-be ex-husband, "I found me." I discover myself through invisible steps by focusing on what matters most and spending my time supporting my priorities. It's not how many hours we work each day. It's about working smarter and prioritizing what is important to us.

Many poems in this book focus on digital technology. Like many, I am working to reduce the amount of time or the frequency I check email or social media for no reason other than to click. Seeing a constant flood of other people's newsfeeds is not always helpful or the best use of our time. A red sticky note rests on my phone with the word "Stop" written on the note. This reminds my brain that I don't need another dopamine hit every four minutes during the day. I think about what it means to be human. To smile. To say hello to others. To write notes. To make phone calls. To focus on the beauty of humanity and to honor the discovery of myself.

Poetry in the Wild

I believe that poetry is best read outside, at the beach, in the living room, or after everyone is asleep. Away from tiny screens, pings, and temptations to check on something that most of the time really does not matter. To be human is to savor the delights of reading a new book or to simply enjoy the quietness of evening or the warmth of the fire with ourselves or someone special.

Poems are wild, beautiful, creative moments caught in the nick of time from our souls. Yet we often debate about how a poem should be written or how much editing needs to be done. A little here, a little there, a complete rewrite--working to conform to a belief system of how poems should be arranged.

The overproduction of the soul. Random rhyming words without thought or introspective observation of the tiny details of life, we carelessly flick away. So much overproduction of our soul's most significant effort.

Acknowledgements

My music muses for *To Be Human –
Always* are SHAED, an amazing indie
band from Washington, D.C., and the
early music of Stevie Nicks and Lindsey
Buckingham. I have a private playlist on
YouTube and listen continuously while I
write. For me, music and writing are
bonded together.

To my editor, Cindy Vallar, whose
encouragement and insight, and kind
guidance helped strengthen my writing –
thank you for all your help.

To my son, Brandon Belanger, a
special thank you for your constant
support and encouragement.

And finally, to the individuals who
randomly crossed my path and provided
encouragement when I needed support
and was afraid to ask – thank you.

About the Author

Tiffany Sunday is a poet, lyricist, and author of *Proper Grey Areas*, *Insatiable Consumption of Being*, *How Dyslexics Will Rule the Future*, *Dyslexia's Competitive Edge*, and *You Posted What!?* She is internationally known for her 2015 TEDx Talk *Dyslexia 2.0: The Gift of Innovation and Entrepreneurial Mind*. Tiffany is based in Dallas, Texas.